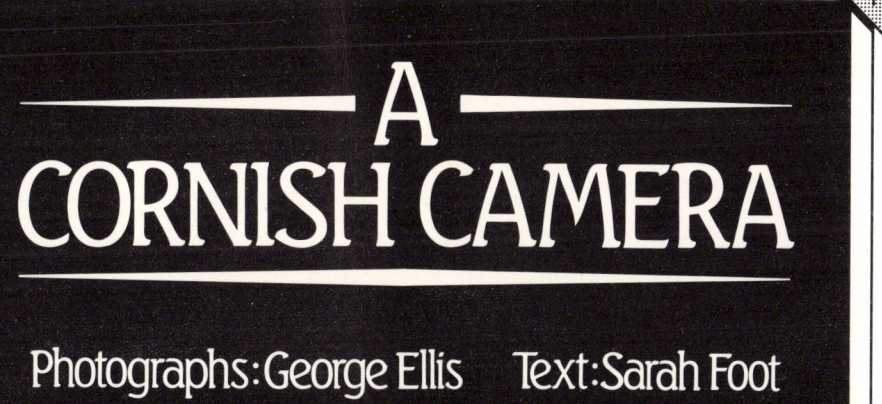

# A CORNISH CAMERA

Photographs: George Ellis    Text: Sarah Foot

**Bossiney Books**

*First published in 1982*
*by Bossiney Books*
*St Teath, Bodmin, Cornwall*
*Designed, typeset and printed in Great Britain by*
*Penwell Ltd, Parkwood, Callington*
*Cornwall*
All rights reserved

*ISBN 0 906456 63 0*

The publishers acknowledge with gratitude the kindness of the management
of the *Cornish Guardian* in allowing the use of photographs taken by
George Ellis during the early months of World War II, when he was in their
employment.

Photo: Paul Broadhurst

The camera can achieve various things. It can capture and record. It can probe and identify. But, above all else, it provides evidence. Much, of course, depends on the man behind the camera. Here then is a unique book, more than 200 photographs taken by George Ellis, the doyen of Cornish press photographers. Cornwall at work and play in war and peace; town and countryside and coast; personalities and customs; triumphs and tragedies: George Ellis has frozen them all in a span of more than forty years — and now in his 80s he works on. The best photographs though often need an interpretation, and Sarah Foot does just that, giving us insights into some of the stories behind these pictures. She loves and cares for Cornwall — and their combined result is a book both exciting and nostalgic.

**George Ellis** (above) looking through some of his hundred thousand negatives which are filed with great efficiency and stored at Bugle. His career as a photographer also seems to have given him a photographic memory and he can remember, in extraordinary detail, events that happened forty years ago. Each photograph he looks at conjures up some sad, thrilling, funny, dramatic or painful memory. It was never too much trouble for him to obtain a really fine photograph. He has become popular with the rich and the famous and loved by the people of Cornwall.

**Sarah Foot** lives at St Mellion. This is her 5th title for Bossiney. In 1981 she wrote the text for *Views of Old Cornwall*, an immediate bestseller, and she is currently working on *The Cornish Countryside*. Her previous titles were *My Grandfather Isaac Foot*, *Following the Tamar* and *Following the River Fowey*.

# A CORNISH CAMERA

When I was first told about George Ellis's collection of photographs I was intrigued. To think of 100,000 negatives covering over forty years of Cornwall's history, all carefully titled, filed and stored away, was overwhelming. Quite naturally I could not wait to see them.

I first met Mr Ellis when I was five years old. I was staying with my grandfather at his house near Callington, when he came to photograph the family, four of whom were preparing to fight in the General Election of 1945. Of course I was too young to realise that it was Mr Ellis who was there but I remember the occasion well. It has made it all the more interesting for me to have had this early connection with the photographer who is now known by so many people throughout Cornwall and who has produced this collection of photographs.

George Ellis came from London to

◄The view from St Juliot Church door showing stone stile and cross, 11 January 1940.

Bodmin the day war broke out to work for the *Cornish Guardian.* He was the only full time press photographer to remain in Cornwall throughout the war, and he stayed on, recording over the next four decades the happenings in this county.

But it was not only the outstanding events and newsworthy stories that he was to search out with his camera, for he also recorded all the nuances that go to make up the character of Cornwall. In an uncanny way he had the rare quality of understanding the Cornish so that he was able to reproduce scenes not only as they were but as they felt.

He told me once that he was warned by friends that he would not find the Cornish easy to get on with or live amongst and quite naturally he and his wife were a little nervous on leaving their London home to make a new life in far off Bodmin. But they both felt welcome and loved the place from the beginning.

Not many 'foreigners' who come to Cornwall find a happy relationship with the people and the place so quickly. But

Above: Sunrise in Mevagissey harbour. George Ellis was already capturing the atmosphere of Cornwall during his first month in the county. Right: Early morning, Mevagissey, taken 13 October 1939.

there have been some who have come, fallen in love with Cornwall, and over the ensuing years become more Cornish than the Cornish and as proud and interested as any Cornishman in the county's history, present and future.

As I have worked with this remarkable collection of photographs taken by Mr Ellis, I have been impressed at his depth of feeling for the atmosphere and character of the place and people. Whether he is photographing the last of the sailing schooners, the little fishing boats of Mevagissey, desolate moorland scenes, farming characters inspecting machinery and animals, Royal visits or annual festivities, he can catch what adds up to the essence of Cornwall, an essence that has eluded many a settler from 'up country'.

While researching stories connected with the photographs, I have come across people who have known George Ellis over the years and all of them speak of him with affection and respect. Some were famous and rich, others more ordinary folk, but they all seem to have fond memories. He, too, remembers Bishops, High Sherrifs and County Councillors, farmers, miners and fishermen with an equal amount of pleasure, interest and understanding.

To work with this combination of a portrayal of history, atmosphere and character has been most intriguing. Though things have undoubtedly changed in the county since the trying and sometimes frightening war years which Mr Ellis captured so poignantly; though buildings and machinery, pastimes, mining, fishing and politics may have altered dramatically over the past forty years, there is, thankfully, much that has not changed. And hopefully these durable qualities of place and people will last another few centuries yet.

Meanwhile here is the story of much that happened in Cornwall during these forty years, many of the people and beautiful places that continue to make the county what it is, captured forever through the lens of George Ellis's camera.

6

In September 1939 there was little
sign that the second World War had
been declared: the North Cornwall
fox hounds met at Blisland with
Captain R.H. Hall as MFH . . .

. . . the first wartime harvest was
brought in at Halgavor, Mr W.
Chapman's farm near Bodmin . . .

. . . and the great waves rolled into Looe beach, washing along the Banjo Pier as they came. George Ellis was already capturing these Cornish scenes.

A three-horse plough at work at Lawhibbet Farm between Golant and Fowey in October 1939. Next to this field lies Castle Dore, the famous Iron Age hillfort, dating from the second century BC, but its real fame comes from the possibility that the Cornish King Mark made his citadel here around 500 AD. So Castle Dore lies at the centre of the Tristan and Iseult legend and the tragedy of their secret love. Such legends have left their romantic mark right across the landscape of Cornwall.

But war had been declared. In September 1939 many soldiers were taking leave of their families and were posted away for service. On 5 September of that year Private Henderson said goodbye to his wife and family at Bodmin. Mr Henderson and his wife are still living in Bodmin today.

**Right:** This young girl's father took a wise precaution in the early weeks of the war. He painted her bicycle white so that it could be seen better in the dimmed lights of black-out. She was photographed by George Ellis as she rode home from Liskeard County School to her home at St Cleer. The girl's name was Doreen Philp and the photograph was taken on 25 September 1939.

Showing a jauntiness and willingness to fight for King and Country, these young soldiers of the Bodmin Terriers display the 'Hitler Wanted' notice on their truck as they leave for service on 5 September 1939.

During the early months of the war every child was given a gas mask in a cardboard box which they were expected to carry with them wherever they went.

This little girl was photographed on Porthpean beach near St Austell in September 1939. One can only wonder who she was. And where is she now?

Showing the resilience of children the second photograph depicts a happy group of youngsters, seemingly unperturbed by the gas masks they all carry, as they leave school in Bodmin in the early weeks of the war.

12

A young evacuee from London is
astonished to find himself gazing into
a car window at a calf! He had only
been in Bodmin a few weeks when
the photograph was taken in
November 1939.

With the constant threat of air raids hanging over them, many people in Cornwall took what precautions they could and dug their own air raid shelters. The photograph above shows Mr Grose of St Austell and a neighbour digging a shelter in their home town.

The South East Cornwall control room was set up in Liskeard during the war for Air Raid Precaution. This photograph of the telephone room was taken in October 1939.

Mr John Rathbone, MP for Bodmin, and his family in the grounds of their house, Elmsleigh, near Par on Boxing Day 1939. A year later Mr Rathbone was killed in action. He had been elected at the early age of 25 and lost his life at 30. After his death his American wife was adopted by the Conservatives as their candidate in the Bodmin division and she became MP in her husband's constituency. The photograph (below) shows Mr and Mrs Rathbone with their son and daughter and the two grandmothers.

Photographer George W.F. Ellis on duty at 'S.3' Royal Observer Post on Bodmin Beacon. Mr Ellis served with the Royal Observer Corps throughout the War. He was also the only full-time press photographer left in Cornwall during the war years.

This was his first home in Cornwall: the Liskeard Road Toll House at Bodmin. It was the registered fever hospital for the area.

Two of George Ellis's sons gathering holly in 1939 near their Bodmin home for the first Christmas they were to spend in Cornwall. Keith is on the left and Cheslie on the right.

Bowling has long been a popular sport in
Cornwall. Here the Looe Bowling Club play a
friendly match of Bowls with Looe Councillors
on 28 September 1939.

Mr and Mrs Samuel Hore, Mayor and Mayoress
of Bodmin, photographed in November 1939.
He was a well-known local businessman who
owned Dennis and Co. Coal Merchants. He
came from a local family who resided at
Laninval House, now part of St Lawrence's
Hospital.

These pictures show the fearful damage done to Falmouth in the air raid of 30 May 1940. One young officer who was staying at the Pentargan and had just arrived in Falmouth to take over his ship was unscathed though his neighbouring room mates were killed. He is seen in the photograph wandering about looking for his belongings amongst the débris in borrowed trousers and rain-coat.

Standing guard over the Nazi Dornier
Flying Pencil which crashed at Boconnoc
near Lostwithiel on Saturday 9 November
1940. All the crew perished.

Young boys investigating the damage in
Padstow caused by the air raid on 5
October 1940.

Captain V.S. Rashleigh presenting the Board of Trade shield for the most meritorious service of 1939 by any Life Saving Apparatus Company to Coastguard Macdonald of Port Isaac and Volunteer R.S. Male of Trebetherick for the saving of three lives from the SS Medea on Greenaway Rocks on 3 January 1939.

In the background are the LSA crews and police officers who assisted in the rescue. The presentation took place in February 1940 and George Ellis produced this composite photograph to commemorate the occasion.

The topsail schooner *Katie* built in Padstow in 1881 moored at Par (left). She was the last of the coastal sailing traders carrying china clay from Cornwall and returning loaded with coal. So it was said of her that she went away white and returned black.

*Katie's* regular passages were to the Thames or Runcorn. However in 1940, soon after these photographs were taken, she was machine-gunned by a German aeroplane in the Irish Sea and brought back to Cornwall where she was laid up in dry dock. In 1947 she was bought by a Danish shipping company and after some repairs she was sailed to Denmark under the new name of *Bargfalk*.

Several years later, with the help of a Cornish preservation society, the *Katie* was taken under tow to be brought home. Unfortunately she was in such a bad state that she sank on the way back and was never recovered.

*Katie* being unloaded at Mevagissey.

Above: Viscount Clifden performing the opening ceremony at the Red Cross effort at Bodmin Cattle Market on 3 October 1940. The auctioneer on the left is Mr Kempthorne Barber and on the right stands the Mayor, Mr Sam Hore. £300 was raised.

Left: Choosing clothes that will be serviceable at an ancient fair at Bodmin called St Lawrence. This fair was originally a horse fair. The picture was taken in October 1939, just after the outbreak of the Second World War.

Perhaps only in Cornwall could it happen that a heifer should give evidence in court.

But that was exactly what occurred in a case that became legendary in the county in November 1940.

It was alleged by a farmer that one of his cows had been stolen by a neighbouring smallholder. The only way that he could prove that this missing cow belonged to him was by displaying the close friendship between the heifer and his cowman Fred Jewell.

So the court adjourned from Camelford County Court to a nearby field wher the cowman called to the heifer and it immediately came over and climbed on Fred's back. On this evidence the case was won.

To the judge's great delight all those concerned ended by shaking hands and the two farmers from Boscastle were once again firm friends. Jenny, the heifer, had settled the matter once and for all.

**Polperro Fishermen, July 1940.**

**A Mevagissey fisherman—July 1944.**

Though it may be a picturesque part of Cornish life, net-mending is an arduous and time-consuming job for all fishermen.

Here fishermen in Mevagissey and at Polperro (left) are seen involved in this task. The pictures were taken in the early 1940s. During the war years there were restrictions put on the fishing fleets. 'Twelve miles south from Looe and twelve miles south from Dodman point' was the limit set, so Mr Eddie Lakeman, a fisherman from

Early morning at Padstow Fish Market, March 1940.

Mevagissey told me. 'When the light went they would put a wire across the harbour at Mevagissey and it was not lifted until sunrise. If we were not in by then we had to stay out at sea all night. Sometimes we were machine-gunned from German planes and we had to be cautious of mine fields.'

Mr Lakeman was taught how to mend fishing nets by his father and he became so expert at it that he would often mend other fishermen's nets for them. 'A lot couldn't mend their own nets,' he said. The fishermen's work was extremely important during the war since food was always short. 'We fished for pilchards, herring and mackerel and in the summer for whiting. We would go out to the full twelve mile extent by day and fish with spiller lines four or five miles long,' Mr Lakeman told me.

The choirs of Cornwall are less famous, perhaps, than those of Wales but are nonetheless enthusiastic and were often drawn from the fishermen and miners of the day.

Below members of the Looe Fishermen's Choir of 1940 pause in their work to discuss with their conductor, Mr Harold Mutton, a new piece of music for their next performance.

One of the strangest sights around St Austell during the war was to see the troops of the Royal Indian Army Service Corps, who were stationed there, out exercising their mule trains. They used the old cinema in St Austell as stables and Mr Ellis recollects seeing the mules being led out of the old Exit doors.

With toy guns, bows and arrows and parachutes made from handkerchiefs these young boys of Bodmin form their own Junior Home Guard in the summer of 1940.

Wadebridge War Weapons Week in May 1941. During the war years parades of this nature seemed to boost morale and concentrate attention on the general war effort throughout the country. Here the Red Cross and Wadebridge ARP Personnel are seen passing the saluting base by Egloshayle playing fields.

In January 1941 Spitfire Week was held in Wadebridge, in aid of the Spitfire fund. The captured Messerschmitt 109 was on view and intrigued the crowd who came.

But the War years did not put a stop to Cornwall's traditional activities. Here (right) the travelling library is visiting the little village of Blisland on Bodmin Moor in February 1940.

At Pawlyn's fish factory in Mevagissey women are packing pilchards into tins. In the last century women in Cornwall were salting pilchards into barrels. Now there are no longer pilchards off the Cornish coast. The photograph was taken in October 1939.

. . . and Curtis's shipyard at Looe turns its hand to building fire floats and other craft for emergency use.

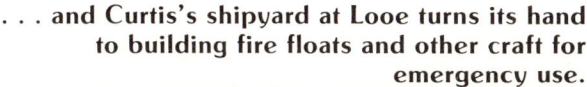

The King and Queen arriving at Liskeard Station on 7 May 1942 and later (below) during the same visit they are talking to the tenants of the Home Farm, Stoke Climsland, one of the farms owned by the Duchy.

HM King George VI walking with Canon Martin Andrews (above) after the inspection of the Home Guard who were assembled in the Rectory grounds at Stoke Climsland on 7 May 1942. Canon Andrews was Rector of Stoke Climsland for 47 years and is one of the best loved characters of this part of Cornwall. He was a friend of the Duke of Windsor when he was Prince of Wales and did much to help during the recession and unemployment of the 1930s. With the encouragement of the Prince of Wales he started a market garden which became a thriving business and he was able to offer employment to many of the local people.

Canon Andrews is now retired and lives at Downderry but at the age of 95 he still preaches from time to time. His warm clear voice and powerful character are undiminished by age or time.

On 7 August 1942 came the terrible Air Raid on Bodmin when nine people were killed. The photographs show: Right: A young woman being rescued from the wrecked offices of the Gasworks. Above: A general picture of the funeral of the air raid victims held on 11 August 1942. Hundreds of mourners attended, while babies in prams were kept at a discreet distance. Below: The Vicar of Bodmin, Father Young, conducting the committal. Eight of those killed in the air raid were members of one family including a small baby.

Waste paper being baled by council employees at Bodmin in June 1940 as part of the war effort. The scene is at the square which is now the shopping car park at the bottom of Bree Shute. Looking on on the far left is Mr Buscombe, Borough Surveyor, and to the right Councillor G.J. Smith.

During the war every available bit of metal was ordered to be scrapped to go towards the war effort. However some pieces of metal were reprieved if they were considered to be of outstanding beauty. These railings outside Abbey House, Padstow were ordered by the Government to be retained. They are still there to this day.

32

Bob Hope was one of several entertainers who came to cheer the US troops at Bodmin. On 15 July 1943 he came to the barracks and in spite of the torrential rain he evidently kept the troops laughing.

Two famous Cornish literary characters. Sir Arthur Quiller-Couch, the author 'Q' of many novels based on his home town of Fowey, and the original editor of the *Oxford Book of English Verse.*

He is photographed on the eve of his 80th birthday on 21 November 1943, in the study of his house, The Haven, overlooking Fowey harbour.

Dr A.L. Rowse the author, historian and poet taken in April 1940 in his study. He now lives in the beautiful house Trenarren, just outside St Austell and overlooking the sea, the house he loved and admired as a boy.

A fogou at Carn Euny in Sancreed. The word fogou is an old Celtic-Cornish word meaning cave. These caves were built by the Iron Age people and there are several fine examples in West Cornwall. Smelted tin, pottery, querns, flints and iron implements have been found in these ancient caves.

They were usually built with very low entrances leading into tunnels, the sides of which are built up with heavy stones and roofed over with large slabs.

Their purpose can only be conjecture, but they could have provided an excellent hiding place for valuables or cold storage for food. On the other hand their purpose may have been ritualistic.

Cornwall's wartime answer to the combine harvester. A three-horse binding machine which was in use at the Riddle's farm, Kingswood, Cardinham on Bodmin Moor in August 1942.

In August 1940 the first Combine Harvester was brought to Cornwall. The photograph shows the new machine being demonstrated to farmers at Mr N. Collin's farm at Pennatillie, St Columb. Their expressions seem to reflect the typical Cornishman's apprehension for new-fangled machinery.

In August 1944 there was a marvellous wartime crop at Helligan on Bodmin Moor. Much of the crop was over 6ft tall.

Harvesting reeds for thatching hay ricks and old cottages taking place on Corgee moor in September 1943. A practice that has almost died out.

Reclamation of moorland for agricultural uses was an important part of warwork in Cornwall. This picture taken in November 1944 shows Cornwall's heaviest and largest plough, which had not been used since World War I, being put back to work on the downs near Castle an Dinas.

On 28 July 1944 Mr R.S. Hudson, Minister of Agriculture, paid a visit to Cornwall and spent some time at Lidcutt, near Bodmin, the home of the Mayor of Bodmin, Councillor Frank Richards. Mr Hudson holds the South Devon bull while Mr Richards looks on.

Miss Anne Taylor, the Champion Landgirl of East Cornwall at South Treviddo Farm, near Liskeard, taken in November 1941.

Before the war Miss Taylor was training for the Ballet Jooss and was at that time shortly to leave with the others on a tour of America. She gave up her career to come to Cornwall and work on the land as so many other women did at the time. She became an excellent practical farmer, and particularly shone in her test for milking; she also ploughed a field at the farm.

Landgirls at Boyton Forestry Camp near Launceston.

Landgirl, Joyce Merryweather, at Great Crugmere Farm, Padstow. She became famous as 'the landgirl who made the Queen laugh' at a Women's Land Army Rally in Hyde Park.

Royal Naval Barracks Boys' Brigade
dance the 'Hornpipe' at Port Eliot, on
4 September 1943, for the St
Germans Fete. The house is now the
home of Lord Eliot, heir to the Earl of
St Germans.

Young RNAS sea cadets at St
Merryn being put through
their paces in pulling and
sailing instruction on Whalers
in the estuary of the River
Camel in May 1944.

Outsize saffron buns were always a feature of the Methodist Sunday School anniversaries. During the war people learned to do without them when bread was rationed. But on 29 July 1944 at Enniscaven, near St Dennis, the Methodist Sunday School made a special effort for their centenary and the huge saffron cakes were once again part of the day, though not everybody appears to approve!

Captain Fredenberger of the US Army appears to be under orders himself from the lady officer in charge of the company of the Girls' Brigade when he inspected the parade at the St Austell Youth Rally in August 1944.

Hundreds of child evacuees were to come to Cornwall during the war years. In July 1944, when the bombing around London became more frequent, these children arrived at Wadebridge from Ewell, Epsom and Worcester Park. They were met at the station by Councillor W. Symons who was then Chairman of Wadebridge Council.

Cornwall is not renowned for its trees, which only makes the wooded areas all the more appreciated by inhabitants and visitors alike. Unfortunately this lovely wooded avenue no longer exists in the grand state the photograph shows it in 1944. All the trees went when a wider road was built on the A30 road from Bodmin to Launceston. The picture was taken just below the present junction of the Launceston and Liskeard roads.

Great excitement took place in Mevagissey in September 1944 when the filming of 'Johnny Frenchman' took place in the harbour and many local people were used as extras.

Many important and famous people visited Cornwall during the war years to give encouragment or in some cases to have a holiday.

In October 1940 the Duke of Gloucester is seen leaving Bodmin police station, (now demolished) with Major E. Hare, Chief Constable of Cornwall.

In March 1944 Field Marshall Montgomery came to Carlyon Bay, Cornwall to visit his old school, King's School, Canterbury, which had been evacuated there for the duration of the war.

Lady Mountbatten inspecting the toys made by wounded servicemen at St Rumon's Hotel, Newquay. It was a sale in aid of the St John Ambulance Brigade which took place on 11 November 1944.

At this time most of the hotels in the area were commandeered for wounded soldiers. Lady Mountbatten became Superintendent-in-Chief of the St John's Ambulance Brigade in 1942 and remained in this position until she died in 1960.

In February 1944 HRH the Duchess of Kent came for a holiday at Trebetherick, near Polzeath, with her three children. Two years earlier the Duke of Kent had been killed in a tragic air crash.

This magnificent photograph of Mr Justice Lawrence arriving at Bodmin Assize court by coach was used on the cover of *The Field* magazine in July 1944.

The old custom of using a coach on such an occasion was reintroduced by Mr John Percival Williams of Lanarth, St Keverne who was High Sherriff of Cornwall that year. The coach belonged to his family and had been used years before by his father when he had been High Sherriff.

In the following year it was used for the last time and, below, Mr Justice Tucker is seen in the Judge's Procession crossing Church Square, Bodmin during Assizes in February 1945.

It was a passage from the Book of Isaiah which inspired The Reverend J.H. Parsons of Liskeard to have two swords fashioned into ploughshares during the second world war. 'And their swords shall be turned into ploughshares'. And this was exactly what happened. One of the swords used was wielded by the Vicar in a cavalry charge in Palestine in 1917 which also brought him the award of the Military Cross, the second sword was that of a Turkish officer whom he captured.

The picture (above) shows the Reverend Parsons ploughing at Mr John Moon's Bolitho Farm near Liskeard with the finished ploughshares in November 1945.

Signposts being replaced at Tresla Corner, Cardinham. A good sign that invasion was no longer feared.

Above: Everyone, in his own way, throughout the British Isles was to celebrate VJ day. Here the Bugle Band leads a procession through the lanes surrounding the china clay district. The photograph was taken in August 1945.

Below: One of the many Victory celebrations in Cornwall — a Tea Time Treat at Wadebridge children's sports on Egloshayle playing fields when hundreds of children and their parents gathered together to celebrate the end of the war. The photograph was taken on 8 June 1946.

Cornwall has long been a place to inspire poets, painters and artists alike.

It was here on the cliffs near Polzeath that Laurence Binyon wrote the immortal lines of his poem, *For the Fallen*, used every Remembrance Sunday to this day:

*They shall grow not old, as we that are left grow old:*
*Age shall not weary them, nor the years condemn.*
*At the going down of the sun and in the morning*
*We shall remember them.*

George Ellis made a postcard of this photograph and sold literally thousands over the years after the war.

The Maypole celebrations in Lanreath and the surrounding villages have a particular twist of their own. Not only are their Maypoles supposedly some of the longest in the world — Pelynt Maypole at 105 feet long was in the Guinness Book of Records for being the longest in the world — but they are also traditionally stolen and taken from one village to another.

These high jinks used to continue right through the month of May and at times things would get out of hand and there would be some heavy fighting. But now the game lasts a shorter time and Maypoles are usually stolen while the guards sleep or leave their duties for other reasons. Lerryn, Dobwalls, St Neot, Lanreath and Pelynt have all been involved in the Maypole escapades over the years. This photograph shows the children dancing round the Maypole at Lanreath in 1946, a particularly important occasion for George Ellis who had encouraged the revival of this custom after the war. He also spotted one of the stolen Maypoles when it was hidden in the woods near Liskeard.

In the summer of 1946 the Freedom of the Town of Bodmin was presented to the Duke of Cornwall's Light Infantry. The photograph shows the regiment parading in Church Square to mark the occasion.

A dramatic picture of the breakwater
and coast at Bude taken in August
1947.

Also in Bude the quaintly named Nanny
Moore's Bridge photographed in 1945.
It was named after a famous widow of
the last century who lived in the
building now called Parson's Bakery.
There was a mill at this bridge which
was worked by the turn of the tide.

Mining for wolfram at Castle an Dinas mine on Goss Moor in 1945. This mine was worked from 1911 until 1956. Recently there has been talk about re-opening the mine as wolfram, a commodity used for strengthening steel, is once more in demand. But though wolfram is mined elsewhere in Cornwall this particular mine remains closed.

The gray slates and clouds of Cornwall. The most famous slate in the world is mined at Delabole on the north coast of Cornwall. The photograph shows the slates stacked in serried ranks waiting to be sent away where they would beautify many a building throughout the country.

In March 1945 the famous BBC recordist of bird sounds Ludwig Koch came to Cornwall to capture the sounds of sea and river. He is seen with Mr Paul Ellingham the senior BBC programme engineer recording sea sounds in Newquay harbour. And on the River Gannel recording different water sounds.

Lady du Maurier, mother of the three du Maurier sisters, Daphne, Angela and Jeanne, at their home Ferryside at Bodinnick, in August 1946. This was the house that the three girls and their mother fell in love with on a holiday visit to the area and which they bought within the next few days. Daphne du Maurier was to write her first book from here and Angela du Maurier still lives there today.

Below: A famous walk above the village of Bodinnick on the estuary of the Fowey River offers some of the finest views in Cornwall. From here you can look across at the town of Fowey and down the coast to Gribbin Head.

It was this magnificent position that was chosen for the Fowey War Memorial pictured here with the fine backdrop of Fowey town.

A family group of the famous novelist Dame Daphne du Maurier taken during the war outside Menabilly, the house she loved and made famous in *Rebecca* renaming it *Manderley.* With her are her three children, Christian, Tessa and Flavia. Her husband was the famous airborne General F.A.M. Browning.

The famous Jamaica Inn on Bodmin Moor which Daphne du Maurier immortalised in her novel of the same name. The photograph was taken in 1948 before it was modernised.

The Cornish Gorsedd when it was held at Launceston in 1947. This event takes place annually in Cornwall when new Bards are initiated.

The photograph shows the 'Fruits of the Earth' being offered to the Grand Bard, R. Morton Nance. The gentleman in white is the Reverend Elvet Lewis, once Grand Bard of Wales.

The first Gorsedd was held in Cornwall in 1928 when a small band of Cornish men and women created the ever-growing fellowship 'to guard and enhance all that is Cornish in our way of life'. Now for fifty four years the ceremony with the blue-robed Bards has been part of Cornish life. Those early Cornish Bards who started the whole movement had the watchwords — *Bedheugh Bynytha Kernewek* — Be For Ever Cornish.

The Gorsedd of the Bards of Cornwall has close ties with such bodies as the Celtic Congress, the Royal Institution of Cornwall, the Institute of Cornish Studies, the Cornish Language Board, the Cornish Music Festival and, of course, the Federation of Old Cornwall Societies from which the original idea sprang. Though the movement is ridiculed by some, others feel it most important that the spirit of Celtic Cornwall should be kept alive and well.

At the St Columb Christmas Fat Stock Show in 1947 Mr S.O. Taylor of Camborne shows off his beast Tehidy Lad which won the prize of 'Best in Show'.

A classic picture of Fore Street, Bodmin, taken in January 1947 looking east towards Turret Clock. Market Street is on the left and also on the left the old Market House columns with cow's heads topping them can be seen above the old Town Arms Hotel building with hanging sign. The Town Arms has now been rebuilt into Bricknell's shop.

The bridges of Cornwall mark some of the most picturesque spots in the county whether they be in towns or in the more secluded countryside.

Two old bridges in Launceston, St Leonard's (below) and St Thomas' (above) are supreme examples. St Leonard's Packhorse bridge once had a deep ford just below it but now it has a wide bridge built over the ford. These pictures were taken in the early 1940s.

Mr John Birch R.A. lived and painted at
Lamorna and thus gained the name of 'Lamorna'
Birch. In 1939 the Queen Mother chose one of
his paintings for her Christmas card and in 1947
he was commissioned to paint two Cornish
scenes as a wedding gift from the people of
Cornwall for Princess Elizabeth and her
husband-to-be, the Duke of Edinburgh. The
photograph shows John Birch painting Respryn
Bridge which crosses the River Fowey just by
Lanhydrock House. This was part of the wedding
gift — he also painted famous Horsebridge on
the River Tamar for the Princess.

Mrs A. Thomas aged 87

Longevity of life has been enjoyed by many Cornish people and old age is properly respected.

Mrs A.J. Best, Mrs A. Thomas and Mrs J.Y. Crowle of St Dennis were all over 80 years old when Mr Ellis photographed them and they were all still practising that particularly womanly craft of knitting.

This craft of knitting was surrounded by folklore in Cornwall when the fishermen's wives knitted the jerseys for their men which had to be warm and weatherproof. Many a woman was to be seen in the fishing villages knitting as they waited for their husbands to return from sea.

Mrs A.J. Best aged 82

Mrs J.Y. Crowle aged 81

Four elderly inhabitants of Trequite, a small hamlet near St Kew. Back row: left Mr Edwin Kellow 91 years; right Mr Nicholas Bray 84 years. Front row: left Mrs F. Taylor 87 years and right Mr Jacob Stone 94 years. They were photographed in April 1940.

Mr Dennis Chaplin became known as the world's 'Oldest Boy Scouter'. He lived in Par and was 89 years old when this photograph was taken in February 1957. He was a well-known character and always appeared at local functions in his uniform.

There are places in Cornwall that are so much an integral part of its character that to see them is to conjure up the spirit of the county which has seduced so many people and rejected others.

Castles, dramatic coastlines, protected river beds, wild moors and steeply banked fishing villages are the places that add up to make Cornwall what it is.

These photographs typify the loved and yet slightly haunting scenes of this Celtic county's beauty.

**Below:** The River Fowey where it runs through the historic town of Lostwithiel. A family of swans with seven cygnets wends its way between the rowing boats.

**Above right:** St Michael's Mount firstly a Celtic Holy place and later used by the monks of St Michael in Brittany. During the Civil Wars it was a Royalist stonghold and in 1660 was bought by John St Aubyn and has remained in that family ever since. The causeway from the mainland at Marazion to the Mount can only be passed at low tide which somehow adds to its sense of mystery.

**Right centre and below:** The Norman Castle of Dunheved at Launceston and the Southgate Archway leading into the town that was once entirely surrounded by walls. This town is still called the Gateway to Cornwall.

**River Fowey, Lostwithiel**

St Michael's Mount

Launceston Castle

Southgate Arch, Launceston

Three Cornish Families:

Firstly: A famous Cornish family of the Church. (above left) The Reverend and Mrs W.G.W. Sara celebrated their diamond wedding anniversary on 28 October 1940. They were living at Avery Terrace, Lostwithiel, but were formerly from St Veep. The Reverend Sara was 84 years old while his wife was 83.

Back row: Mrs C.G. Sara, Revd. W.G.W. Sara, The Rt. Revd. Edmund W. Sara, Asst. Bishop Bath and Wells (youngest son) Mrs G.S.C. Sara.
Front row: The Revd. Claude G. Sara, Rector of St Deny's (eldest son), Mrs W.G.W. Sara, Mr Gerald Sara of Calgary, Canada (second son).

The Foot family, famous in political life, gathered (below left) in the dining room of Mr Isaac Foot's house, Pencrebar at Callington.

Four members of the family were preparing to fight the 1945 election. Mr Isaac Foot at Tavistock, Mr John Foot at Bodmin, Dingle Foot (not present) at Dundee and Mr Michael Foot at Devonport. They were all Liberal candidates except Michael who was Labour and only he was successful.

At the head of the table sits Mr Isaac Foot and to his left Mrs Hugh Foot now Lady Caradon; Jennifer Highet (Isaac's daughter); Mr John Foot now Lord Foot; Mrs Isaac Foot, Mr Hugh Foot now Lord Caradon; Mrs John Foot now Lady Foot; and Mr Michael Foot sits on his father's right.

A famous Cornish wrestling family (above) taken at Mount Wise, Newquay, in August 1945.
Left to right: C. Chapman, of St Wenn, belt holder; W. Chapman of Tremoor, winner all weights and heavy and boy champion; J. Chapman of St Wenn four times lightweight champion; H. Hawkey (cousin of the Chapmans); S. Chapman also of St Wenn; F. Tippett a promising lad of twelve years from Colan.

A heady mixture of coastline and bulbs which can be seen in parts of Cornwall during the springtime. This particular landscape at Broom Parc, Portloe near Veryan is a particular favourite with George Ellis and his family. They make a pilgrimage there every year at Easter time. This photograph was taken in April 1952. The property is now owned by the National Trust.

The thatched, white-washed round houses of Veryan. They were known as 'devil scarers'. Some of them owe their existence to the Reverend Jeremiah Trist who in the early part of the last century had them built and topped with crosses to keep the devil away. Their circular shape symbolised the continuity between God and Eternity and would offer no corners for the devil to hide in.

In the 1940s a new set of round houses were built in Veryan. They were provided from the legacy of the will of Miss Maria Kempe Homeyard and were allocated to the widows of seamen with the stipulation that first consideration should be given to the widows of Cornishmen.

Mr Reg Dyer of St Austell was a famous yachts-
man who twice entered the Fastnet Race and was
a regular contestant at Cowes and other yachting
centres. He is seen at the helm of his 12 metre
yacht *Flica 1* during a race from Fowey to
Falmouth. His yacht was laid up during the war
years but he refitted it for this race which took
place in August 1946. Two years later in August
1948 he was washed overboard on a visit to
Cowes.

There are many stories of sea tragedies taking
place in Cornwall even with such experienced
yachtsmen as Mr Dyer. Those who live near the
sea and sail on it have learned never to under-
estimate its danger.

In April 1948 Mr Richard
Dimbleby, probably the
country's most famous
radio and TV broadcaster,
came to Bodmin to record a
programme in the 'Down
Your Way' series. He is
seen trying on the Town
Crier's clothes for size.

67

**Helston Furry Dance**

**Children's Dance at Helston**

**St Luke's Methodist Church
Sunday School Treat at Dozmary
Pool on Bodmin Moor.**

There are many annual festivals held in Cornwall which have been part of the county's way of life since time immemorial.

The Helston Furry Dance is perhaps the best known of these. It is celebrated every year on 8 May and these photographs were taken on that occasion in 1950. They show the children's dance and the Mid-day Dance in which only invited guests can take part and they must wear top hats and tails for men and Ascot dresses for the ladies. The dancers wend their way in and out of the houses of the town and the town band plays the well-known tune of the Furry Dance.

Another famous festival is that of the Padstow Hobby Horse which is held on May Day each year. The custom is of very ancient origin dating from

Padstow May Day Teazer and Horse.

Junior Horse and Teazers in Market Square.

pre-Christian times. The horse is led through the town by the 'teazer' and to the accompaniment of music from the accordion. The photographs were taken in 1948 and 1949.

Annual events celebrated every year throughout Cornwall are the Sunday School Anniversaries. This one was the St Luke's Methodist Church treat. This tiny church on Bodmin Moor was once always packed on Sundays with farmers who often walked for miles from their lonely farms on the moor to attend the services. In 1953, as in other years, their Sunday School treat was held at famous Dozmary Pool on Bodmin Moor and a motorboat was brought from Looe for trips on the lake and the band played beside the water.

The Duchess of Kent launches
the new Padstow Lifeboat in 1952

Cornish people are probably prouder of their
lifeboat crews than any other section of their
society. Never a year goes by without their pride
being justified with feats of skill and bravery.

In May 1952 the Duchess of Kent came to
launch the new lifeboat at Padstow and is seen
chatting to the crew. Her son and daughter-in-
law, the present Duke and Duchess of Kent, have
recently done much to raise the spirits of the
families of the crew of the Penlee lifeboat who
lost their men in a dramatic and brave attempt to
save the crew of *Union Star* which had gone
aground on the rocks near Mousehole.

Lifeboatmen are understandably proud of their
medals and the photograph on the left taken in
December 1945 is of Bill Orchard, Padstow
lifeboat mechanic, displaying his medal.

70

When the Royal Cornwall Show was held in Callington, on Duchy property in July 1950 it was also the occasion for a Royal visit. King George VI, Queen Elizabeth and Princess Margaret all attended. The photograph shows the Queen and the Princess arriving at the Women's Institute Tent.

During the same visit to Cornwall, the Royal party visited Bodmin. The Queen leads the way having been greeted by the Mayor, Mr W. Stanley Smith. She is followed by the King and the Princess.

Gwennap Pit is an amphitheatre carved out of a hollow formed by land subsidence from the mining in this area. John Wesley preached here and in his eighty fifth year it was said that he had a congregation of twenty thousand people.

Now, on Whit Monday, every year there is a great gathering of Methodists with some of the finest preachers in the land coming to give their sermons. This photograph was taken on Whit Monday 1950.

The Reverend Donald Soper, now Lord Soper, the famous Methodist preacher, speaking in the pulpit of the Port Isaac Valley Church in 1953. The Church is no longer in existence.

Members and friends of the Emmanuel Methodist Church at Indian Queens celebrated their centenary year by dressing up in Victorian fashions. Many of the clothes were family heirlooms. The gentleman in the top hat is the Reverend Thomas Shaw, the church minister.

Political Visitors to Cornwall — The Rt Hon Harold Macmillan (centre) at Liskeard Conservative Rally on 10 June 1949. To the left is Douglas Marshall then MP for Bodmin District who was later knighted, and to the right is Mr R.J. Couch of Looe.

In January 1953 Mr Clement Atlee (right) leader of the opposition visited St Austell and was welcomed at the Public Rooms by Mr Frank Hayman MP (Labour — Falmouth Truro).

On 28 April 1973 the large and famously outspoken Liberal MP, Mr Cyril Smith paid a visit to Launceston. With him in the picture are Mr John Pardoe, at that time Liberal MP for North Cornwall, with his wife and Mr Peter Cocks of Newquay.

For many years the Roman Catholic Archbishop of Westminster, Cardinal Bernard Griffin, came to holiday on one of Cornwall's most beautiful stretches of coastline at Polzeath. He preferred to remain anonymous during his visits and would often attend service in the Catholic Church at Bodmin, sitting discreetly in the back pew.

Sadly in August 1956 when he was staying at Winwalde, Polzeath (the house shown in the photograph) he died suddenly. An open air service of absolution was held outside St Mary's Abbey, Bodmin where the cortege stopped, though the coffin never left the hearse, but continued onto Ealing where the funeral service and burial took place. The lower photograph shows Abbot Aloysius Smith by the cortege and Monsignor Derek Worlock, the Cardinal's secretary, standing by the pavement.

The story of the American vessel, the *Flying Enterprise*, was one so immersed in mystery and bravery that it caught the imagination of people throughout the world.

It was just after Christmas in 1951 that the 6,711 ton *Flying Enterprise* got into trouble in bad storms 300 miles out into the Atlantic.

A Falmouth tug *Turmoil* went out to find her. On 29 December the brave Captain Kirt Carlsen ordered all passengers and members of the crew off the ship. Each member of the crew took charge of a passenger and they jumped into the icy sea where they were picked up by other ships, including an American destroyer.

From that date until 4 January Captain Carlsen remained alone on board his ship with radio contact to the tug and destroyer. He found it difficult to move about the ship because of her severe list and found only one beaker of fresh water and some beer to drink and fruit cake to eat. On the 4 January when the tug came close to the ship to try to attach a tow line the tug's mate Kenneth Dancy, aged 27, was able to leap on board.

Meanwhile heavy cloud prevented a helicopter helping in the rescue operation. When a line was eventually attached the *Flying Enterprise* was towed 250 miles towards Falmouth but in worsening weather the line broke.

Despite repeated attempts to save the *Enterprise*, her Captain and Kenneth Dancy eventually had to jump from the funnel of the ship just minutes before she went down. The two men were rescued by the tug and taken back to Falmouth to a heroes' welcome.

But the story did not end there for there was tremendous speculation about what cargo the

*Flying Enterprise* was carrying. It was reported that she was carrying motor cars, coffee, mail from Germany for the USA and other general cargo. But later reports divulged further information. A diving operation 18 months later was said by a Russian journal to have salvaged six mystery boxes alleged to contain instruments of high military value.

Then according to reports from Brussels an Italian salvage firm recovered about £35,700 from the ship which was under 240 feet of water 50 miles off the Cornish Coast.

Later 1,500 watches were salvaged from the vessel. Then £50,000 of stocks and shares as well as banknotes were found by the salvage company. Captain Carlsen was reputed to have commented when told of the finds, 'If I had known anything about it I would have been a nervous wreck.' The president of the firm who owned the vessel said some of the items had not been listed as part of the ship's cargo.

So the mystery remains. The end of the story was that *Turmoil*, the tug that had stayed with the ship and spent five days trying to bring her back to Falmouth and so nearly succeeded, was paid nothing for her endeavours. She, like most tugs, had been employed on a 'no cure, no pay' contract and although the crew had saved the lives of the Captain and their own mate they were not compensated.

George Ellis remembers going out by fishing boat in frightful weather to get this photograph and being warned off by the crew of an American destroyer. However in the early light of dawn he took his photograph which was widely used in many newspapers throughout the country.

Shipwrecks on the Cornish coast then are, sadly,

HMS *Warspite* grounded near St Michael's Mount

not a thing of the past. These three photographs are further witness to the tragedies which happen all too frequently.

In March 1947 the *Empire Contamar* drifted at anchor in Par Bay and hooked up on the rocks. When the tide went out her bottom was smashed. Happily the crew were saved and most of the cargo salvaged.

By ingenious methods the ship too was eventually salvaged by the bilge being filled with concrete and the water being pumped out. She was eventually sailed back into Fowey harbour.

The HMS *Wave* also dragged her anchor while sheltering in St Ives Bay. The picture was taken in October 1952. The ship ended upright inside the harbour near the Lifeboat Station on the rocks. It was safely towed off at high tide a few days later.

The hulk of the HMS *Warspite* is shown grounded near St Michaels Mount after breaking its tow in May 1951.

HMS *Wave* on the rocks at St Ives

*Empire Contamar* in Par Bay.

A picturesque setting for a back-breaking task, broccoli gathering with Gulval Parish Church in the background.

Another picturesque setting for picking broccoli at Gulval, Mount's Bay with St Michael's Mount, one of the most famous of Cornish landmarks, in the distance. The picture was taken in 1951.

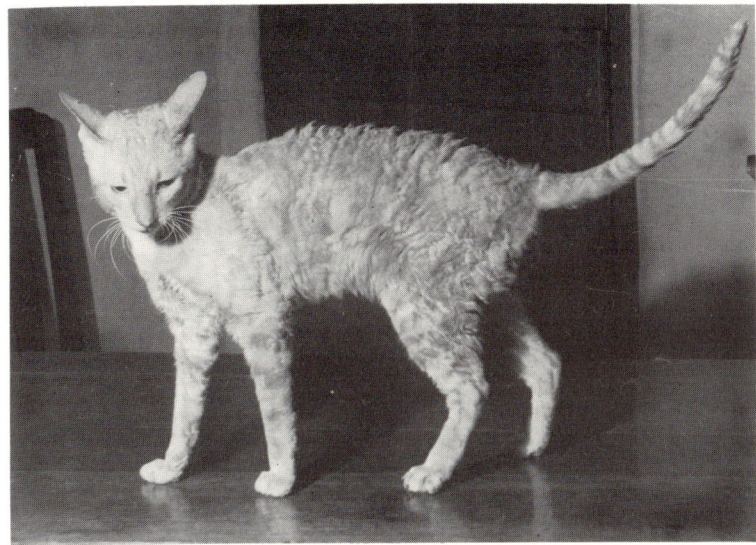

The cat that started the Cornish Rex breed. It was found in 1950 in a litter of kittens from a tortoise house cat and a wild Tom cat. Mrs Ennismore of Seven Stars, Bugle, who was the owner, was attracted by the unusual fur which was very closely curled, even the whiskers were curled. On advice from a geneticist, Kallibunker, the original kitten, was mated with his mother and two more Rex kittens were born. Eventually some of the Rex cats were sent to America and Canada where the breeding continued.

Once the Rex cats were officially recognized there was a constant demand for them and a popularity poll in 1970 showed them as second only to the Siamese.

Many unusual plants, some of a tropical nature, are grown in Cornwall. These giant American Aloe trees, which flower only once in a lifetime and then die, were growing in Mrs Whittle's front garden in St Blazey. The two trees had grown there for some years but in September 1953 they both decided to flower and the stalks shot up until they were as high as the roof. They died during the following winter.

Prince and Princess Chula of Thailand at their home, Tredethy, near Helland Bridge with Thailand naval cadets in June 1953. Prince and Princess Chula bought the house just after the war and stayed there until they died. They were extremely popular members of the community and gave generously to the town of Bodmin.

They had one daughter, Narisa, born in August 1956 and photographed here by George Ellis one month after her birth.

The Prince died when he was only 55 years old in 1963 and Princess Chula died in 1971 when she

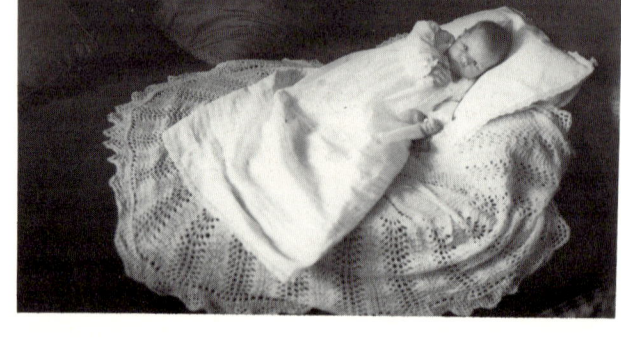

was also 55 years old. Their daughter is now married and lives in London and the house, Tredethy, has been sold and has become a hotel.

During the war a Mrs Wilson J.P. lived there and turned the house into a sick and convalescent home for Londoners. Later when it became the home of Prince and Princess Chula, Prince Bira, their cousin, often stayed there. He was a famous racing driver.

The Opening Meet of the East
Cornwall Hounds at Minions near
the Cheesewring on Bodmin Moor
on 3 November 1953. Major J.
Lethbridge was MFH.

The agricultural shows of Cornwall are a way of
life. The greatest of them all, of course, is the
Royal Cornwall Show which is visited annually
by almost every farmer in the county. Children
take time off from school, wives from their
chores and farmers from the fields and stock to
gather for the event.

But each district's local agricultural show is
important to the country way of life and each has
an atmosphere entirely of its own.

Here the grand parade of champions is taking
place just before the prize giving at Camelford
Agricultural Show on 29 July 1961.

Ann Todd, the famous film star at her home Glendorgal, near Newquay sitting on the rocks with her dog, Peter. The photograph was taken in July 1946 when she was the wife of Nigel Tangye.

Lady Mander unveils a memorial stone to John Whitehead Peard in Fowey churchyard in August 1957. Colonel Peard lived at nearby Penquite House overlooking the Fowey River near Golant. He was a great friend of Garibaldi's and joined him in his Austrian campaign in 1859. In 1864 Garibaldi came to stay with Colonel Peard at Penquite and was to cause quite a stir in this part of Cornwall where crowds gathered everywhere to see the famous General. In St Austell most of the shops were shut and a holiday announced so that the people could gather along the route that Garibaldi was to travel.

Above: Miss Dorothy Dudley, a well-known archaeologist, directing excavations at Garrow Tor on Bodmin Moor in June 1952. Miss Dudley started a new career in her sixties in Cornwall after retiring from teaching. It was a career which brought her great success, her most important excavations being at Nornour in the Isles of Scilly and at Tregiffian, St Buryan. She died in 1975 in her ninetieth year.

Many famous writers and artists have been attracted by the beauty of Fowey town and come to live, write and paint there.

Arthur Quiller Couch belonged there, Daphne du Maurier came there as a girl, wrote her first book there and lived there for many years. Kenneth Grahame wrote part of *Wind in the Willows* there and Mabel Lucy Attwell (shown below) lived in Fowey for many years and was pictured there in December 1957.

Cornwall is famous for its mild climate but now and then the county experiences really cold winters with heavy frosts, snow and ice.

In 1954 Mr Everett, a Bodmin plumber, was overwhelmed with requests to mend burst pipes in the bitter February of that year. His lists (above) were chalked up on slates in his work room.

Seven years earlier in 1947 Police Sergeant Snell (top left) was photographed near Bodmin Post Office during the snow.

And snow ploughs were hard at work in the same year on Bodmin Moor. The photograph (below left) was taken in January at Helland village.

On 14 November 1957 Prince Philip had a busy day visiting St Blazey, Par and Melbur. The day ended watching a football match at St Blazey where a special 'Royal Box' had been constructed for the Prince.

In 1962 the Queen and Prince Philip paid one of their many popular visits to Cornwall. Here she is seen walking through Lostwithiel after visiting the Vicarage. She is with the Mayor of Lostwithiel, the Reverend Albert Sykes. Mrs Sykes is between Prince Philip and Mr Hawken, a retired schoolmaster.

Old age does not necessarily mean that hands must become idle. Here are two elderly gentlemen to prove the point. Mr H. Tregilgas. (above right) a famous and popular character of Bodmin, looked after the gardens opposite Bodmin Parish Church known as Robartes Gardens. This photograph was taken in May 1940 when Mr. Tregilgas was 90 years old. The gardens disappeared when the road was widened and re-aligned.

Mr Thomas Philp of Pennant Farm near Blisland was photographed (above left) at the age of 94 in August 1956 shocking corn.

Tom, Dick and Harry, three old bowling veterans at the Poltair Bowling Week in August 1953. They are Tom Old of Newquay Trenance Club, aged 79; Dick Tremberth of Poltair Club, St Austell aged 86 and Harry Bidgood of Poltair Club aged 71.

A cloam oven that was still in use in 1957. The photographs show Mrs Tamblin of Botelet, Lanreath firing her oven in preparation for a day of baking.

Cornwall is famous for its dramatic views of sea
and cliffs, but when these are enhanced by the
river estuaries they are even more breath-taking.
The estuary of the River Camel is one of the
most beautiful in the county and to look down to
it from Pentire Point is to see a panoramic view
without rival.

Oyster fishing at the Duchy of Cornwall Oyster
Farm at Port Navas on the Helford River. The
fishermen can be seen hauling in the dredges
which they have drawn across the oyster beds.
This is a time-honoured occupation for fishermen
in this area and one that is still practised today.
The photograph was taken in September 1955.

Preparing for the annual Harvest of the Sea Service at Mevagissey Congregational Church in October 1960. Mr Chris Cloke and Mr Ambrose Pollard, two local fishermen, are seen working on the model fishing boat with its drift nets and silvered cardboard fishes which formed the background of the setting for the service.

The fiddler leading the procession to the Knill Monument at St Ives. This ancient custom still takes place in memory of one of St Ives's great characters. John Knill, who was born in Callington in 1733 and had a remarkable career which included becoming a bencher at Gray's Inn, secretary to Lord Buckingham, a Commissioner for the inspection of ports in the West Indies and finally Mayor and collector of customs at St Ives.

He built a 'folly' in the shape of a pyramid just outside St Ives and left an annuity instructing the mayor to make sure that every five years there would be celebrations in the town in his memory. The celebrations include ten girls from St Ives, dressed in white who sing and dance to the music of a fiddler.

The ceremony of the Boy Bishop was once celebrated all over the country. It is a medieval custom which has been resurrected from time to time.

In 1953 the ceremony was performed at the Good Shepherd Church at Par (above) and was an annual event for about eight years after. It was believed to be a good way of capturing children's interest in church services by letting them take part in the ceremony. The boy elected to be Bishop would be expected to help with altar serving throughout the year and to give an example of good churchmanship to his contemporaries. The custom has now died out in Cornwall.

At the annual ceremony of Ringing in the New Year at Bodmin (below) it is traditional that the Mayor 'Rings the old year out at midnight'. In December 1956 the Mayor was Mr R. Dawe and he can be seen sitting in the window on the right waiting to perform this time-honoured task.

This photograph (left) was taken in March 1960 during the enthronement of the 10th Bishop of Truro, Bishop John Maurice Key.

The Cathedral was built in the 1880s on the site of the former Parish Church of St Mary and part of this Church is incorporated into the Cathedral building.

The architect J.L. Pearson died during the building of the Cathedral and his son continued the work, following his father's plans as closely as possible.

The Rt Revd Edmund Morgan who became Bishop of Truro photographed in June 1951.

The Midsummer Eve Chain of Bonfires and Crying the Neck are two ancient Cornish customs which died out in the latter part of the last century and have been revived in the 1920s by the Old Cornwall Societies.

The Midsummer Eve Bonfire celebrations are believed to have taken place across the county on prominent hill tops since pagan times. The bonfires were originally kindled by Druids on their sacred places on the 1st May each year and were a form of sun worship and a blessing on the crops and animals.

As with so many old pagan customs the bonfires were later incorporated into Christian festivities and they are now lit to celebrate the Eve of St John's Day. In the latter part of the nineteenth century the custom entirely died out, but in 1929 the bonfires were once again lit starting at Chapel Carn Brea overlooking Land's End followed by others at Castle an Dinas and Rosewall Hill with the chain running on through eighty miles to Kit Hill on the Devon border.

In heathen times animals and criminals were sometimes sacrificed on the bonfires. Now the Lady of the Flowers casts a bunch of herbs bound with ribbon into the fire as seen in the above photograph which was taken at St Breock Downs in 1961. Angela Toms was the Lady of the Flowers on this occasion. As the herbs are thrown into the

fire the following words are recited:

*In one bunch together bound*
*Flowers for burning here are found,*
*Both good and ill.*
*Thousandfold let good seed spring,*
*Wicked weeds, fast withering;*
*Let this fire kill!*

'Crying the Neck' was also a pagan custom that was adopted in a different form by the early Christians. Once the custom was worldwide and survived in Devon and Cornwall until the latter half of the nineteenth century.

The ceremony consists of the last sheaf of corn being cut by the oldest reaper. It is then held aloft to the cry of 'I have 'et' three times. The others say 'What have 'ee' three times. And the answer comes 'A Neck! A Neck! A Neck!' Then all say 'hurrah' loudly three times. The neck is then plaited and decorated with flowers and taken home to be hung in the farmhouse on the beam until the next harvest. In the modern day celebrations sometimes the sheaf is carried to a church or chapel where a thanksgiving service is then performed.

M.A. Courtney in *Cornish Feasts and Folklore* wrote: ' . . . the ceremony was simply to give notice to the surrounding country that the harvest was ended.' And Lady Vyvyan of Trelowarren in

*Our Cornwall* quotes an old man as saying, 'a 'andsome sound it was to hear the Neck cried come harvest time. You could hear they cries all over the county in every direction.'

As with the Bonfire Celebrations there seems little doubt that originally Crying the Neck derived from a sacrificial ceremony, the victim being the embodiment of the Corn Spirit. The custom of killing the Corn Spirit apparently originated 7,000 years ago in the Middle East.

The photograph below shows the occasion in September 1961 when the Helston Old Cornwall Society helped to revive the custom. Mr Reginald James Freeman is 'crying the neck'. On his left is 79 year old Mr J. Waters.

Some say the ancient sport of Hurling dates back as far as the Bronze Age. Certainly many of the old Cornish legends are interwoven with stories of Hurlers and Hurling. Carew of Antony wrote about Hurling in 1602 in his famous *Survey of Cornwall*.

Now it is resurrected every Shrove Tuesday in the town of St Columb and on the Saturday of the following week.

Rules have differed over the years, once in the west of Cornwall the silver ball was hurled until it crossed the parish border. In the east of Cornwall it was hurled, or dealt, towards a goal. One thing that is certain it is not a game for the faint of heart or weak of limb. The teams are made up of country people against the town folk and the motto of hurling still holds true: 'Fair play is good play'.

I like C.E. Vullaimy's description in the 1920s best. 'Across the slopes of the Moors, and through the fields beneath them, the men of Cornwall used to play their game of Hurling, the manliest most glorious and exciting game that was ever played in Britain. It was an Homeric Game, a game fit for heroes . . .

These photographs (above) of Hurling at St Columb were taken in 1964.

**Two Intrepid Women Walkers  (John o' Groats - Land's End) and their Menus for meals in a Cafe at Bodmin, Cornwall.**

## DR. BARBARA MOORE
56 YEAR OLD VEGETARIAN
JOHN O' GROATS          JANUARY 13th.
LAND'S END              FEBRUARY 4th.

MENU:  LETTUCE, BROCOLLI, CARROT, CELERY, CHICORY, TURNIP, TOMATO, NUTS, RAISINS, OLIVE OIL, HONEY, CORNISH CREAM, ORANGE JUICE.

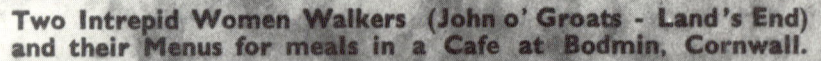

JOHN O' GROATS

1960

VINTAGE
YEAR
FOR LONG
DISTANCE
WALKERS
Approximate
Distance
900 Miles

LAND'S
END

## WENDY LEWIS
18 YEAR OLD HAIR STYLIST OF LIVERPOOL
JOHN O' GROATS          JANUARY. 14th
LAND'S END              FEBRUARY 7th.

MENU:  STEAK AND KIDNEY PIE, POTATOES AND GREENS, PEACHES, ICE CREAM, CORNISH CREAM, PASTIES, SAFFRON CAKE, CYDRAX, TEA.

During an exercise for army cadets at Perranporth in August 1961 DUCKWS are seen against a background of huge waves going in to land an attack on Perranporth beach.

The Duke of Edinburgh boarding his helicopter of the Queen's Flight as he prepares to leave St Austell Grammar School grounds after a visit in May 1961.

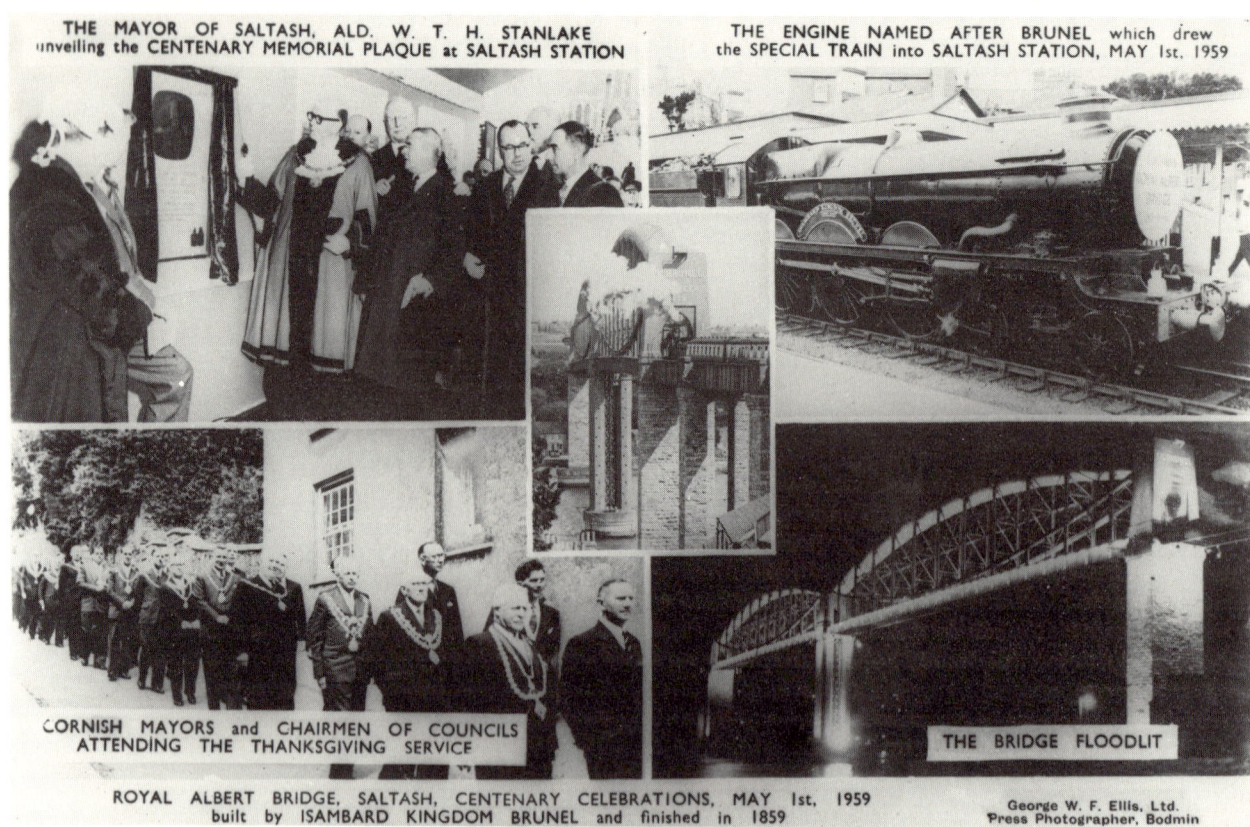

THE MAYOR OF SALTASH, ALD. W. T. H. STANLAKE unveiling the CENTENARY MEMORIAL PLAQUE at SALTASH STATION

THE ENGINE NAMED AFTER BRUNEL which drew the SPECIAL TRAIN into SALTASH STATION, MAY 1st, 1959

CORNISH MAYORS and CHAIRMEN OF COUNCILS ATTENDING THE THANKSGIVING SERVICE

THE BRIDGE FLOODLIT

ROYAL ALBERT BRIDGE, SALTASH, CENTENARY CELEBRATIONS, MAY 1st, 1959 built by ISAMBARD KINGDOM BRUNEL and finished in 1859

George W. F. Ellis, Ltd. Press Photographer, Bodmin

THE LAST DAY OF SALTASH FERRY, OCTOBER 24th, 1961. It is moored at Saltash Ferry Gate with Brunel's famous ALBERT BRIDGE for the Railway opened in 1859 framing the new Saltash Road Bridge across the River Tamar, now in use. Inset is a picture of the Old Saltash Horse Ferry about 1830.

George W. F. Ellis, Ltd Press Photographer, Bod

In October 1961 when the Saltash bridge was first opened to the general public the first horse was led across. The bridge was to change the life of people living in Saltash with the tremendous increase in traffic from across the water. The easy access to Plymouth encouraged many people to live in the riverside town who could now easily commute to the Devon city for work. The one time fisher town was never to be the same again.

The official opening of the Saltash Road Bridge took place on 26 April 1962. Queen Elizabeth, the Queen Mother, performed the official ceremony and is seen unveiling the plaque to commemorate the occasion. The then Lord Lieutenant of Cornwall, Colonel Edward Bolitho, is seen standing on the left of the plaque and Sir John Carew Pole stands on the right.

This photograph of the famous gallery at Lanhydrock House was taken for Viscount Clifden to use as his Christmas card in 1947. Lord Clifden gave the house to the National Trust in 1953 but continued to live there until his death in 1966.

The remarkable plaster barrel ceiling is believed to have been finished before the outbreak of Civil War in 1642. The room, which is 116 feet long has perfect acoustics and is often used for musical evenings with great success.

Left: The gateway to Lanhydrock House showing its marvellous wooded setting in the Fowey valley. The house was originally built by a merchant from Truro whose family later became great benefactors to the community and during the Civil War were Parliamentarians. Later they became Liberal politicians of great popularity.

Caerhays Castle, one of Cornwall's most famous beauty spots. The castle was designed by John Nash in 1808 and is surrounded by some of the most beautiful grounds in the county. The Trevanion family built the castle and it is now the home of Mr Julian Williams who is the Chairman of the Cornwall County Council. The Williams family once owned vast mining interests throughout the county.

The prehistoric tumuli and standing stones used to be the landmarks of Goonhilly Downs but now it is more famous for the huge satellite 'dishes'. It was here that the first transatlantic television pictures were received.

One of the 'Dishes' (left) can be seen through the window of the control tower at the Satellite Communication Ground Station. In the other photograph (far left) one of these strange constructions is shown close up. It is 85 feet in diameter and weighs 870 tons with the base. It is no wonder that these monsters dominate the whole desolate landscape. The photographs were taken in 1962.

A dramatic picture of the Commando Ridge at Bosrigan, near Zennor where the Boys' Brigade had a special camp in conjunction with the Cornwall County Council Youth Department in August 1961. This was part of their rock climbing course.

The site was so named because the British Commando troops trained there during World War II.

The Church of St Juliot which is often referred to as the Thomas Hardy Church. It was the great writer who helped to restore the Church in 1872 and rebuilt the north aisle during his earlier career as an architect.

There is a wall tablet in the north aisle which he set up for his wife who was related to the Vicar of the Church at the time when Hardy was working and living in the area. It was while he was living here that he wrote *A Pair of Blue Eyes* and many of his finer poems. In 1928 when Hardy died there was a memorial tablet erected in the Church detailing his close connection with the building.

Sunlight filters through into the crypt of St Thomas à Beckett Chantry Chapel at Bodmin. The photograph was taken in October 1939.

In June 1962 the bells of Bodmin Church were re-cast and re-hung. The photograph shows the number 7 bell, the second largest, being guided through the belfry window. The window framing had previously been removed to allow the bells to be taken down and then replaced. In the foreground can be seen the framework on which the bells were eventually hung.

105

The Golden Jubilee of Biscovey School, Par on 23 May 1962. Andrea Rundle was the 50th Queen of the May at the ceremony of that year and she can be seen seated with her attendants during the Maypole dancing in the Dell by the school.

Cornwall has grown used to the threat and actuality of floods over the years. In 1963 there were severe floods in North Cornwall like those shown in the photograph at Mill House Inn in Trebarwith Valley. Local inhabitants including Councillor Fred Whiting, now of Tintagel, seem to be bearing the drama with wry good humour.

**Mount Folly, Bodmin, looking down Turf Street**
This characteristic little Cornish slate building
was demolished in 1963 (below) to widen the
road for modern traffic.

Two photographs show the keen interest and close association that Michael Cardew, the famous potter, had with African potters. In 1952 African Chiefs and foreign students (above left) visited his pottery at Wenford Bridge near Bodmin Moor and watched him throw a pot in his workshop.

In 1962 a Nigerian potter (below left) demonstrated her method of pottery to Michael Cardew and Bernard Leach, probably the most famous potter of them all who had been Michael Cardew's teacher. He is seen sitting third from right. In this Nigerian method of pottery the pot is built up from long rolls of clay which are then smoothed by hand. The potter then makes a rhythmic dance round the stationary pot smoothing the clay as if it were on a potter's wheel. Mr Cardew took a great interest in African methods of pottery just as his old teacher Bernard Leach had taken a deep interest in Japanese methods.

Pottery has long been a favourite art form in Cornwall. At Lake's pottery in Truro in April 1944 a potter is seen (above) putting the lip into the rim of a pitcher he has just thrown. This pottery at Truro can be traced back 200 years and has recently been bought by Mr Dennis Hills who intends to keep it going and also to re-vamp the adjoining museum to depict the history of pottery in Cornwall over the years.

**Three aerial views of Cornwall taken in
August 1965.**
   **The patchwork quilt of Cornwall's coastline
at Polkerris. The more urban coastline of
Newquay beaches. And the beautiful last
reaches of the River Fowey unspoilt by the
ships that come to load china clay.**

**River Fowey**

**Newquay**

111

Eccentric and artistic characters seem to thrive in Cornwall. Lauri Smith is such a one. He arrived in Cornwall in 1968 looking for 'peace and freedom' and has found it on Bodmin Moor in a pretty little stone cottage which he has renovated most expertly using granite from a nearby quarry.

He is one of the few leather craftsmen in this country who works largely on medieval leather vessels and has reconstructed such items as a bombard (the largest vessels shown in the picture) the costrel (a leather bottle) and the Black Jack, from research he has done for many years. Some of his work is now displayed in Westminster Abbey, Shakespeare's birthplace in Stratford-upon-Avon and other museums throughout the world.

He also works on modern tooled leatherwork for belts, handbags and bellows. But his talents do not end there. He also works with stone, wood and metal. Having left school at a very early age he has educated himself and is as he says 'in love with the sound of words'. He can recite great reams of poetry and prose and is an ardent reader of philosophical works.

The freedom he was searching for and has found on Bodmin Moor means he can choose his own activity each day. Either to stride across the moor, to sit and discuss world affairs and attitudes with others, or to work away in his workshop on some new piece of art.

The 'Fair Mo' was an ancient pig fair at St Ives. The event continues without the pigs but 'fairings', the famous Cornish biscuits, are still sold. This photograph taken in November 1963 shows Alderman and Mrs E.P. Curnow, the Mayor and Mayoress, sampling the biscuits.

Prince Charles, Duke of Cornwall, seen talking to children and senior citizens at Priory Park, Bodmin during a visit in June 1970. He thrilled both children and adults alike when he arrived in a helicopter at the park.

The new County Hall at Truro which was completed and put to use in 1966. Previously the headquarters of Cornwall County Council had been housed at Station Road in a granite building built in 1912.
The new hall was designed by County Architect, Alan Groves, and was considered to incorporate all that was best and most exciting in modern architecture. The photograph was taken in August 1965.

Sir John Betjeman photographed at his home at
Trebetherick near Wadebridge on the day it was
announced that he had been appointed Poet
Laureate in October 1972.

Pupils and teachers of Mount Charles School, St Austell, visiting the Tall Ships just before the race that started from Plymouth in April 1976. The children are seen leaving the *Christian Radich* one of the square rigged ships that took part in the race. The start of the race from Plymouth Hoe was one of the most dramatic sights the harbour had seen for many years.

The well-known folk group 'The Spinners', recording a programme for the BBC on the Town Quay at Fowey in June 1974.

Mevagissey Feast Week, a very popular and long established event which takes place in July. This photograph was taken in 1976 on the quayside during the community hymn singing.

The ceremony in April 1979 marking the twinning of Bodmin and Le Relecq-Kerhuon in Brittany. The Mayor of Le Relecq-Kerhuon, Guy Liziar, signs the twinning document watched by Councillor L. Smith, Mayor of Bodmin, and Mr Allis, Town Clerk of Bodmin. The twinning idea between Brittany and Cornwall has become so popular that there are sometimes as many as 800 French children and their teachers visiting Cornwal at one time.

In September 1981 the European Flag of Honour was presented to Bodmin by Mayor Francis Tanghe of Ravels, Belgium. The Mayor of Bodmin, Councillor Reginald Lees-Barton, is seen receiving the flag. The presentation was to mark the success of Bodmin twinning with Bederkesa in North Germany for over twenty years and also the twinning between Le Relecq-Kerhuon in Brittany with Bodmin.

The idea of twinning towns was started soon after the war when it was believed that a greater understanding between the people of Germany and Britain would be promoted through regular visits of school children. It proved to be an enormous success and now towns all over the country are linked to similar European towns and regular visits are made by school children from one country to the other. Mr John West, the County Youth Organiser of Cornwall in the 1950s, was the instigator of the twinning system in Cornwall and started such exchanges in the early 1950s.

In May 1981 a party from Bodmin were invited
to their twin town of Bederkesa in North
Germany to present a town flag. The oldest
member of the twinning association was Mr
George Ellis who is seen on the left holding the
flag: on the right is Mrs Mary Haliday, former
mayor of Bodmin. The picture was taken with Mr
Ellis's camera by a German photographer.

In August 1977 the Queen paid a Jubilee visit to Cornwall. This picture was taken at the Royal Cornwall Showground at Wadebridge where many uniformed organisations and young people greeted her. The St John Ambulance Brigade flag dips in salute.

Because the village school of Port Isaac was built at the top of the cliffs, football was never allowed in the playground. To compensate there were four pairs of stilts in the school, with a rota for use during lunch hour. The picture was taken in 1975 when this village school was still in use.

Cherry blossom in all its glory in the Tamar Valley. Once over 40 varieties of cherries were grown in the valley and were famous all over the country. These particular cherry trees are in a creek just above Halton Quay, less than a mile below the house where I live.

Now, though the cherries are no longer grown commercially, many of them remain to adorn the steep slopes that lead down to the River Tamar. Surrounded as they are by the strip market gardening of bulbs, they help to make up one of the most picturesque and colourful parts of Cornwall during the spring time.

# ALSO AVAILABLE

## FOLLOWING THE TAMAR
by Sarah Foot. 63 photographs and map.
Sarah Foot is the Tamar's inevitable author, living only a mile from its banks, seeing it every day from her Cornish home, and truly loving it.
'. . . both a labour of love and a work of subtle selection, combining the intriguing byways of local history and geography with a profusion of well-chosen black and white plates.'
Dick Benson-Gyles, The Western Evening Herald

## MY GRANDFATHER ISAAC FOOT
by Sarah Foot. 58 photographs.
A true crusader, Isaac Foot was a radical, uncompromising Liberal, a staunch Methodist and an eloquent orator and lawyer.
'. . . a rich harvest of information.'            Cornwall Courier
'. . . entirely enchanting . . .'       Alan Gibson, The Spectator
'An affectionate account . . .'            The Sunday Telegraph

## LEGENDS OF CORNWALL
by Sally Jones. 60 photographs and drawings.
Brilliantly illustrated with photographs and vivid drawings of legendary characters. A journey through the legendary sites of Cornwall, beginning at the Tamar and ending at Land's End.
'Highly readable and beautifully romantic . . .'
Desmond Lyons, Cornwall Courier

## KING ARTHUR COUNTRY in CORNWALL, THE SEARCH for the REAL ARTHUR
by Brenda Duxbury, Michael Williams and Colin Wilson.
Over 50 photographs and 3 maps.
An exciting exploration of the Arthurian sites in Cornwall and Scilly, including the related legends of Tristan and Iseult, with The Search for the Real Arthur by Colin Wilson.
'. . . provides a refreshing slant on an old story linking it with the present.'
Caroline Righton. The Packet Newspapers

## MY CORNWALL
A personal vision of Cornwall by eleven writers living and working in the county: Daphne du Maurier, Ronald Duncan, James Turner, Angela du Maurier, Jack Clemo, Denys Val Baker, Colin Wilson, C.C. Vyvyan, Arthur Caddick, Michael Williams and Derek Tangye, with reproductions of paintings by Margo Maeckelberghe and photographs by Bryan Russell.
'An ambitious collection of chapters.'
The Times, London

## STRANGE HAPPENINGS IN CORNWALL
by Michael Williams. 35 photographs.
Strange shapes and strange characters; healing and life after death; reincarnation and Spiritualism; murders and mysteries are only some of the contents in this fascinating book.
'. . . this eerie Cornish collection.'
David Foot, Western Daily Press

## FOLLOWING THE RIVER FOWEY
by Sarah Foot. 49 photographs.
Sarah Foot follows the Fowey from its beginnings on Bodmin Moor to where it meets the sea beyond Fowey and Polruan.
'She stitches into the simple tapestry of the river's story names and incidents and anecdotes, deftly and lovingly, every thread and every page touched with charm and an unashamed sense of delight.'            Western Morning News

## VIEWS OF OLD CORNWALL
by Sarah Foot.
Nearly 200 old picture postcards from the Peter Dryden collection, with text by Sarah Foot, all combine to recall Cornwall as she once was.
'. . . will be certain to start the talk flowing of days gone by.'
The Cornishman

## CORNISH CHURCHES
by Joan Rendell. 60 photographs and drawings.
Here in her fifth title for Bossiney Joan Rendell explores many of Cornwall's lovely churches. Music and myths, art and architecture, personalities past and present are only some of the facets of her journey across the Cornish landscape.
'. . . an author who is well qualified to take us on a tour of Cornish churches . . . extremely readable.'
The Cornish Guardian

## THE CRUEL CORNISH SEA
by David Mudd. 65 photographs.
David Mudd selects more than 30 Cornish shipwrecks, spanning 400 years, in his fascinating account of seas at a coastline that each year claim their toll of human lives.
'This is an important book.'
Lord St Levan, the Cornish Times

## CASTLES OF CORNWALL
by Mary and Hal Price. 78 photographs and map.
St Catherine's Castle and Castle Dore both at Fowey, Restormel near Lostwithiel, St Mawes, Pendennis at Falmouth, St Michael's Mount, Tintagel, Launceston and Trematon near Saltash. Mary and Hal Price on this tour of Cornwall explore these nine castles.
'. . . a lavishly illustrated narrative that is both historically sound and written in a compelling and vivid style that carries the reader along from one drama to the next.'
Pamela Leeds, The Western Evening Herald

## CORNISH MYSTERIES
by Michael Williams. 40 photographs.
Cornish Mysteries is a kind of jig-saw puzzle in words and pictures. The power of charming, mysterious shapes in the Cornish landscape, the baffling murder case of Mrs Hearn are just some fascinating ingredients.
'. . . superstitions, dreams, murder, Lyonesse, the legendary visit of the boy Jesus to Cornwall, and much else. Splendid, and sometimes eerie, chapters.'
The Methodist Recorder